6 Tough (But True) Lessons About Business

BY MICHELLE CELESTIN

6 Tough (But True) Lessons About Business

MICHELLE CELESTIN

StoryTerrace

Text Sharita Hanley, on behalf of StoryTerrace
Design Mitar Stjepcevic, on behalf of StoryTerrace
Copyright © Michelle Celestin and StoryTerrace

Text is private and confidential

First print October 2022

StoryTerrace

www.StoryTerrace.com

CONTENTS

	DEDICATION	7
1.	A BELLE GLADE GIRL WITH BIG DREAMS	9
2.	KNOW YOUR WHY	13
3.	YOU'VE GOT TO DO THE NITTY, GRITTY DIRTY WORK	21
4.	WHEN IT COMES TO FUNDING, GET CREATIVE	27
5.	NETWORK WITH ALL, BUT TRUST FEW	35
6.	BE WILLING TO BE YOUR OWN VILLAGE	41
7.	YOU NEED A STRONG, DETERMINED, AND PERSISTENT MIND	47
8.	NEVER STOP BUILDING	53

DEDICATION

I would like to dedicate this book to:

- My mom Emily Rolle, the hardest working woman I know, and my dad, Donald Brown. Both of them are in heaven smiling down on me.
- My children Oneika, Oneil, Omar, and Kayla who I worked hard for. I became a better person for you all and I hope I've inspired and helped you in some ways so you can continue to be great and an inspiration to others as you embark on your own lives. I am proud of each and every one of you.
- My sisters, Bernice and Stephenie, and brothers, Frankie and James.
- My granddaughter Ke'mora. Keep shining. The world is yours to conquer.
- Nevaeh, my niece that I mentor in my organization. You are such a smart young lady and I know that no matter what career path you choose, you will be successful and do great things.
- Everyone who has ever supported me in my endeavors. I would like to say thank you and love you all.

Starting from left to right Omar, Oneika, me, Kayla and O.Neil.

1

A BELLE GLADE GIRL WITH BIG DREAMS

"No matter where you're from, your dreams are valid." - Lupita Nyong'o

Most kids who grow up in a single-parent home like I did, dream about their parents getting back together, going to Disney World, or getting a new toy. I, who always marched to the beat of my own drum, dreamed about owning a home. It's not the only thing I dreamed about, but growing up in Belle Glade, Florida, a rural, poverty-stricken small town, made me long for something different.

I wanted a better living situation than the two-bedroom apartment my mother, brothers, sisters, and I lived in. I wanted a better job than the ones the city I grew up in offered. I wanted to do more and be more. I was a Belle Glade girl with big dreams.

My dreams grew even bigger when I joined my high school's modeling club which, in many ways, changed my life.

6 TOUGH (BUT TRUE) LESSONS ABOUT BUSINESS

Before I joined the modeling club, I was a tomboy. I was ashamed to walk like a girl. I loved wearing jeans and tennis shoes, but in modeling club, we had to wear dresses and swimsuits. To my surprise, one day, something just clicked for me. I don't know how or why, but I said *I'm going to go for it. I'm going to walk like a lady* and I did. From that point on, I started dressing differently. But the way I dressed wasn't the only thing that changed. My mindset started to change as well.

We went to different schools to perform and model so I got chances to see different places outside of where I lived. I didn't fully understand the environment I lived in until I traveled outside of it and beyond it. I loved where I came from but Belle Glade was a poverty environment. The only ways to make it out were through graduating from high school, receiving a scholarship, or going to college. Modeling club was an eye-opener for me.

Mrs. P, our mentor treated us like we were her kids. She told us we could go and do whatever we wanted to do. She reminded us that there was a great big world out there. She told us not to settle. She told us to dream big. And I did.

I dreamed of being a homeowner, an entrepreneur, a mentor, a leader, and a changemaker. I've accomplished those dreams, but the road hasn't been easy. It's been paved with blood, sweat, tears, perseverance, and a determined mind. Here are some of the experiences and tough, but necessary lessons I've learned along the way.

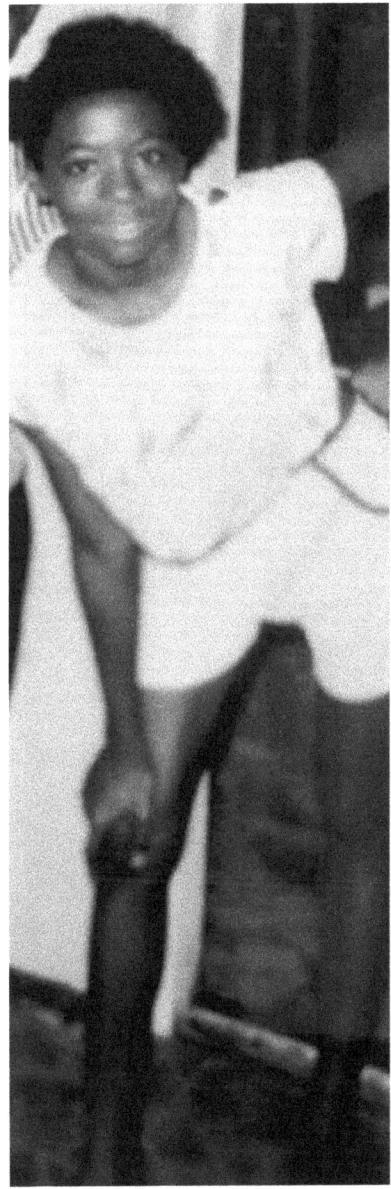

Me when I was about 10 years old.

2
KNOW YOUR WHY

"If you can't figure out your purpose, figure out your passion for your passion will lead you right into your purpose." Bishop T.D. Jakes

Lesson one? You've got to know your why. The thought of being your own boss and building something up from the group can be irresistible, but being a business owner isn't for the faint of heart. It gets hard and business ownership comes with a unique set of challenges.

Not only do you have to come up with a good business idea, but you also have to find the resources to get it off the ground. And even if you are successful in starting your business, you have to deal with the day-to-day challenges of running your organization. From managing finances and staff to marketing your business and dealing with customers, there is a lot to think about. So when the going gets tough and having a business is more work than it is fun, how are you going to stay motivated to keep going?

Every time I felt the urge to give up on my dream, I remembered my why.

Your why is what convinces you to get out of bed in the morning. No matter what your "why," is, it's important to keep it at the top of your mind as you pursue your goals. Why? Because when you know your purpose, it becomes easier to stay focused and stay on track. Your why also gives you something to fall back on when times get tough. And believe me, owning and operating a business, gets tough. So ask yours, what is your "why." Why do you do what you do?

It's a simple question, but it's one that often many people ignore when they think about entrepreneurship. Most people think about money, fame, success, and having a platform. But the best business and most influential business owners have a sense of purpose that drives them. When you know what motivates you, and what your goals and ambitions are, you'll be better equipped to overcome any obstacle that shows up on your path. So get real, raw, and honest with yourself and figure out your why. Then use that knowledge to pursue your dreams.

My why is two-fold. It is both personal and communal. Like most people, it began with a dream that grew into something much, much more.

For as long as I can, I dreamed of owning a home. I wanted my children to live and grow up in a nice place and stable environment. I wanted to keep them away from any and all negative influences as much as I could. But as I'm sure you know, life rarely goes as planned.

My kids started hanging around the wrong crowd. I immediately took action. I started cutting those relationships from the get-go. I didn't even give the relationships time to see where they would go because I knew where I came from. I also knew the kind of trouble kids from my city got into.

I love Belle Glade, but it can be a tough place to live. There is a lot of poverty there and violent things happen often. A lot of the violence happens because the city has a poverty rate of nearly 40%. The majority of people in Belle Glade are hard-working, law-abiding citizens who are just trying to make a better life for themselves and their families. But some residents turn to drugs and criminal activity as a way to cope.

I didn't want that happening to my kids. But I knew how easy it is for kids to succumb to peer pressure. So I told my kids to work hard and protecting them became my primary focus.

They were my why.

But something in me made me think that maybe running these kids off wasn't the answer. Maybe they didn't know any better. Maybe these kids came from a single-parent household like I did. Maybe they were dealing with other issues.

As much as I wanted to protect my own kids, I also wanted to be there for these other kids. I wanted to try to be a positive role model for them. So I said to myself, *instead of turning these kids away let me see if I can help.*

Helping them became my why.

So I started a mentoring organization and in many ways, that's what started my life as a businesswoman.

**

In 2012, I started Women of Sure Sertainty, a non-profit organization whose mission is to encourage young girls to start and run their own businesses through mentoring, education, and training. My vision is to stimulate and encourage the next generation of young female business leaders by creating ONE GIRLPRENEUR AT A TIME.

I meet with the young Women of Sure Sertainty once a month. We talk about different topics ranging from college, healthy and unhealthy sexual activity, establishing a career, bullying, being a leader, and their dreams and visions for their lives.

We have vision board parties. We go on college tours. We visit career fairs. We were at a healthcare job fair when my daughter Kayla realized she wanted to be an anesthesiologist assistant.

We do a lot of work but we also chill, relax, and have fun. Sometimes, we'll go to Golden Corral and share a meal together.

Thanks to a partnership with the WNBA, I also have a basketball camp for girls between the ages of 7 and 14 years old. It is called "Her Time to Play" and the camps are designed to teach kids the basics of basketball, while also instilling important values such as teamwork and sportsmanship. Children in the camp also learn lessons from WNBA players about self-confidence and having a healthy lifestyle.

Both of my organizations are free to attend. Nothing about creating them and maintaining them has been easy, but I continue to do the hard work because I'm driven by my why.

I want to see my kids and kids from my neighborhood thrive, achieve their goals, and become leaders in this world.

Women Of Sure Sertainty photo shoot.

WNBA Jr. nba Her Time To Play Basketball Camp 2021.

Women Of Sure Sertainty Youth Entrepreneurship Summit 2021 Riviera Beach, FL.

3

YOU'VE GOT TO DO THE NITTY, GRITTY DIRTY WORK

"A dream doesn't become reality through magic. It takes sweat, determination, and hard work." - Kevin-Prince Boateng

Once you know your why, you've got to be willing to do the nitty-gritty work. Business owners and entrepreneurs are ambitious, driven, and passionate. But if I'm honest, these qualities aren't enough to guarantee success. Business owners also have to be willing to do the hard work necessary to make their dreams a reality. This means you have to be willing to work long hours, make sacrifices, and constantly challenge yourself to improve. It's not easy, but it's what separates successful entrepreneurs from the rest.

If you're thinking about starting your own business or becoming an entrepreneur, you need to know that hard work will be a part of the journey. Ambition, drive, and passion will get you started, but hard work will be the key that helps you achieve your goals.

Day in and day out you'll need to hustle to get your business off the ground. You need to be constantly networking, selling, and marketing your products or services. You'll also need to wear a lot of hats, from accountant to CEO. And you'll need to do all of this while continuing to be a present and productive member of your family.

I won't lie - doing the nitty gritty work of entrepreneurship as a single mother wasn't fun. It was hard. But I did it and I'm a better woman, mother, leader, mentor, and business owner because of it.

Not long after graduating high school, I moved to Miami, FL. Even though I was married at the time and my husband and I had big dreams, we eventually broke up and I became a single mom. In what felt like an instant, my life changed.

I moved to West Palm Beach, FL and started working as a medical assistant. But as I realized that the money I was making wasn't going to buy me a home. I knew I had to go back to school. In the meantime, I kept doing my job and did the nitty gritty work to make sure my dreams came true.

One day as I went downstairs for lunch, I stopped by a mortgage company located in the building and asked a man working there, "what do I have to do to buy a home?" Even though I desperately wanted to own a home, I was clueless about how to make it happen. I was a single mother with small children just trying to survive.

"How's your credit," the mortgage broker asked, responding to my inquiry. "The first thing you need to do is find out how your credit is. Call these numbers and visit these websites to get free copies of your credit report. Once you get the report, take a look at what's on there. Positive and negative."

I didn't really understand what he was saying so I was like, "Huh?"

He was like, "I can show and tell you what to do when you get your credit report. I can tell you what to look out for, how to dispute them or you can bring your credit report to me and I can charge you and do it for you."

I was like, "Umm, just tell me what to do." So he did. He showed me what to do. I got my credit report, did the nitty gritty work, and figured it out. I cleaned up my own credit report. I was either disputing a discrepancy on my credit report or paying down debt. I sacrificed buying a lot of things to pay down debt but come hell or high water, I was going to buy a home.

Around this same time, I decided to go back to school to be a surgical technician. For the next two years, I worked my butt off and got my associate's degree in surgical tech.

Going back to school can be a tough transition, especially if you've been out of the education system for a while. You have to juggle work and family commitments, but you also have to get used to a new routine. You'll need to budget your time carefully and make sure you're staying on top of your studies. You'll have to dedicate time to homework and studying, but you also have to be present for your family. It is a lot of hard work, but the effort is often worth it. Going back to school can help you gain the skills and knowledge you need to improve your chances of success.

While I worked, went back to school, and cleaned my credit report, I was still a single mom doing the best I could. Some of my kids were in sports, but I planned things in advance and had everything on a schedule. The schedule kept me going. I didn't focus my thoughts on the fact that I was doing a lot, I just did it. I didn't worry about how I was going to do it. I knew that as long as I did the work and stayed on schedule, things ran smoothly, and I was good.

Eventually, my hard work paid off and I got into Section Eight. But I didn't let that slow me down. I learned that Section Eight had a first-time homebuyers program. Once I finished school and began working as a surgical tech, I let the people at Section Eight know that I wanted to join the program. They explained the program to me and luckily, I got in. Right when I joined the program, the housing market crashed. It was the perfect time for me to buy a home.

There was this one housing development that caught my eye as I drove back and forth to school. It was so nice. As I drove back and forth to school I kept telling myself *One day it's going to be me. One day, I'm going to buy a house in there.* My sister Bernice and I actually went in there one day to look around and see the houses up close. I remember telling my sister, "I'm going to live here one day. I don't know how, but one of these houses is going to be mine."

A couple of years of the nitty gritty hard work passed by but eventually that work paid off. I found my house in the place I always said I wanted to live in. And I've been living here in this house for twelve years.

Most businesses and achievements start out as a dream. Whatever your dream may be, you need to know that it will take hard work to make it a reality. You've got to be willing to do the nitty gritty hard work. You have to be willing to put in the long hours or make the sacrifices necessary to make your dreams come true. It's not easy to achieve success, but it's worth it in the end. It won't be easy, but it will be worth it. So don't give up on your dreams. Roll up your sleeves and get to work making them a reality.

4

WHEN IT COMES TO FUNDING, GET CREATIVE

"Start where you are. Use what you have. Do what you can." - Arthur Ashe

One of the most important aspects of running a business is funding it. There are several traditional ways to finance a business and each one has advantages and disadvantages.

Many aspiring business owners plan to take out a loan from a bank. Most people like this option because it provides a large sum of money upfront, which can be really helpful for start-ups or businesses that are growing rapidly. But getting a business loan is usually easier said than done. Banks are often reluctant to give loans to small businesses and entrepreneurs that don't have a track record or collateral. There is also a fair amount of paperwork that needs to be completed before you can get a business loan.

You'll need:
- A detailed business plan
- Information about your company's history, current financial situation, and future goals
- Financial statements such as tax returns
-

Once you've gathered all the required materials, you'll need to fill out a loan application. This will give the lender an overview of your business and help them determine your creditworthiness. If everything goes well, you'll soon be on your way to getting the funding you need to grow your business. But loans also have to be repaid, with interest. If you don't have the money to repay a loan, this process can become extremely stressful and burdensome.

Another traditional way to fund your business is to seek out investments from investors. There are both ups and downs to dealing with an investor. On the upside, an investor can provide much-needed capital for your business. They can also bring enthusiasm and fresh ideas to the table. However, they may want too much control over your business, or they may not be committed to the long-term success of your company. On top of that, some investors may not have the same vision for your business that you do.

Some business owners finance their companies themselves with personal savings, credit cards, and small business grants. This approach can be slower and more challenging than seeking outside funding, but it often allows entrepreneurs full control over their business.

When it came to funding Woman Of Sure Sertainty, I got creative. I used what I had to get what I wanted. I knew how to do credit repair because I learned how to do them from the mortgage broker. The knowledge was great but I needed to find a way to make money from it. So I used my resources and took a credit repair training with a lady I found on Facebook. I took the training and learned all about the credit repair business. That training inspired me to use that knowledge to create an LLC and credit repair business.

I started marketing myself and putting myself out there and people started coming. I wasn't anywhere near a big credit repair business, but I was getting clients here and there. Although I was seeing some small level of success with my credit repair business, funding Women of Sure Sertainty was a struggle. Even though my organization was a non-profit, I wasn't really taking advantage of that fact. I was funding everything on my own or asking my coworkers for help. I would tell them about events I was planning for the girls and ask them if they could provide food or supplies for the event. Thankfully, many of them supported my endeavors and gave me things.

When I decided to apply for grants, I was getting turned down. It was frustrating. I kept thinking *why can't I get a grant?* But the reality was that there were 1,000 other people trying to get grants so there was a lot of competition. But I didn't give up. I got creative.

I had the idea to combine my credit repair business with my 501c3. I realized that the majority of people seeking out credit repair want to buy a home. That's the number one thing they want to buy. But oftentimes, the cost of credit repair deters people. But I wasn't really trying to make money from credit repair. I just wanted to help people buy a home because I know how much joy I experienced when I purchased my own. I wanted everyone to experience that joy. So I decided to offer free credit repair to people looking to improve their credit scores. The only thing they have to do is make a donation to my organization in any amount they choose.

Instead of robbing Peter to pay Paul, I used Peter to help pay Paul. It was a win-win but it all happened because I wasn't afraid to get creative.

As an aspiring business owner, it is essential to be creative in order to succeed. This means thinking outside the box, being proactive, and taking risks. It is also important to have a clear vision for your business and be able to articulate it to others. Being creative doesn't mean that you have to have all the answers, but it does mean being open to new ideas and willing to experiment, especially when it comes to funding your business. Get used to thinking outside the box.

The most successful businesses are those that are constantly evolving and finding new ways to grow. So, if you're feeling stuck, remember to think creatively and take some chances. It could be the key to making your business goals a reality. Tapping into your creativity can be a major asset in your journey as a business owner.

DO YOU NEED YOUR CREDIT REPAIRED AND WANT TO HELP A GOOD CAUSE AT THE SAME TIME? CONSULTING

Palm Beach Credit Repair and Consulting has partnered up with Women Of Sure Sertainty a 501c3 non-profit organization to offer free credit repair services for a DONATION ONLY to anyone who needs their credit repaired. Your tax exempt donation will be helping young girls ages 10-21 years old our program consist of:

Michelle Celestin
Founder & CEO of Women
Of Sure Sertainty

- Entrepreneurship Training
- Financial Literacy Training
- Leadership Training
- Once a month mentoring meetings
- College Tours
- Jr. NBA Her Time To Play basketball camp
And so much more.

I merged my credit repair company with my organization to offer free credit repair to fund my organization.

When it came down to getting creative I starting making my own Women Of Sure Sertainty Body Butter.

5
NETWORK WITH ALL, BUT TRUST FEW

"Be careful who you trust. The devil was once an angel." - Ziad Abdelnour

In today's business world, networking is more important than ever. Networking events provide an invaluable opportunity to meet potential clients and collaborators. In addition to increasing your chances of making a sale or forming a partnership, networking can also help you to develop new skills and knowledge. By speaking with other professionals and aspiring entrepreneurs, you can gain insights into best practices about your industry and learn about new trends. If you attend enough networking events, you'll develop a wide network of contacts that you can call when you need advice, assistance, or simply want to have a conversation about owning a business.

But you don't have to network in person. In the modern world, digital networking is increasingly important. With so much of our lives taking place online, we need to connect with others in a variety of ways. Social media platforms like Facebook, Twitter, and LinkedIn can help aspiring entrepreneurs build business connections.

    I actually met a lady on Facebook to learn more about grant writing. Even though some of her responses were a little rough around the edges, she seemed like she was helping people get grants and grow their businesses. So I joined her grant writing Facebook group. One day, I reached out to her, introduced myself, and told her about my organization. She said she could definitely help me get some grants for Women of Sure Sertainty. Since this was my first time trying to hire a grant writer, I didn't really understand how the process worked, but she sent over her contract. She charged an up front fee of $2,000 for unlimited grant writing for a year. In addition to that, she would get a little percentage of any of the grant money I received. I didn't know too much about grants so I was like, "Okay, cool." She sent over the contract and I signed it.

    After I signed the agreement, she said, "I'll get back with you in about two weeks." I knew she had more clients ahead of me so I had no problem waiting the two weeks.

    When two weeks passed, I reached out to her. "Hey, are we ready to start working on the grants?"

    She responded back saying, "Hey Michelle, I have people ahead of you. Let me work on their stuff and then I'll get back with you." I knew what it was like to work with multiple clients, so I waited another month and a half before reaching out to her again.

At this point, I would text her say, "Hey, you ready to start?" She would respond and say *not yet but I'll be ready to start soon*. I started to realize that I kept getting a lot of *not yet* and *start soon* messages.

Surprisingly, I heard from her one day. She asked me if I had a DUNS number. I didn't really know what that was. "What is that?"

"Oh don't worry about it, I'll set that up for you." So I was like okay. She then said, "In the meantime, you can do some fundraising and stuff like that." I let her know that I did do that and that I also received donations from coworkers and friends.

After explaining that to her, I had one simple question for her, "What's going on with these grants?"

"Well you know, a Bank of America grant just opened up. There's a two-month turnaround." It looked like she started working on the grant, so I waited two months to see whether or not I received the grant money. But she never finished her work on the grant so my application didn't go through. Occasionally, she asked me to fill out a questionnaire or two, which I always did, but ultimately, nothing came out of my time working with her.

At that point, I started to research the grant writing process for myself. I learned about in-kind donations businesses can get. I went back to her and told her about those donations and asked her to apply for them on my behalf. I also asked her to apply for some Walmart grants for me. She refused.

"No, no, no. Those grants are too small. I apply for big grants. I like to apply for the $50,000 and $100,000 grants."

"But I'll take any grant," I responded. Any grant money I received would have been more than I had. But she would never do it. I kept pushing the issue and she would say she was going to do it, but she never did. Unfortunately, this back and forth and lack of progress went on for a whole year. That of course, was the length of my contract.

A year went by and I eventually realized what happened. I was scammed. And that's when I learned that even though entrepreneurs should network with as many people as they can, they should only trust a few.

As an aspiring business owner, you need to network with people. However, it can be difficult to know who to trust, especially when you are first starting out. Here are a few signs that you can look for when you're trying to figure out whether someone is trustworthy or not.

1. They have a track record of success: If someone has a proven track record of success, they are more likely to be trustworthy. This is because they have already navigated the challenges of starting and growing a business, and they know what it takes to overcome obstacles.

2. They are transparent: Transparency is key when it comes to building trust. If someone is open and honest about their intentions, goals, and experiences, it will be easier for you to trust them.

3. They have your best interests at heart: A trustworthy person will always have your best interests at heart. They will be supportive and helpful, rather than trying to take advantage of you or your business.

4. They are knowledgeable: When you are entrusting someone with your business, you want to be sure that they know what they are doing. Look for someone who is knowledgeable and experienced in the field, so you can be confident that they will make sound decisions for your business.

5. They are reliable: Finally, reliability is critical when choosing who to trust in business. You need to be able to rely on someone to follow through on their commitments and deliver on their promises. If someone consistently fails to meet deadlines or meet your expectations, they are not likely to be trustworthy.

When you do network, find someone who shares your values. This will help ensure that they have your best interests at heart and are not simply trying to push you in a certain direction for their own gain. You should also look to connect with people who have experience in the field you're interested in. They will be able to provide you with valuable insights and advice based on their own knowledge and expertise.

Learn from everyone you meet, but remember to only trust a few.

6
BE WILLING TO BE YOUR OWN VILLAGE

"If nobody knocks on your door, knock on your own door! The most precious support for you is the support you give yourself!"- Mehmet Murat Ildan

Most people believe that it takes a village to create a successful business. For many people, that's true. But it doesn't have to be. You can start a business and be successful on your own. Don't get me wrong - being a business owner can be a lonely experience, but you need to learn how to count on yourself in times of need or distress.

Being a business owner can be tough. There are going to be good times and hard times, especially when you're just starting out. That's why you need to learn how to be your own support system. You've got to be your own cheerleader. You need to be comfortable figuring things out on your own.

Because there are so many facets to running a business, learning to be self-reliant can be a daunting task. But you have to be willing to take care of all aspects of the business, from the day-to-day operations to the long-term strategic planning. You also need to be willing and able to handle all the challenges that come with owning a business such as financial difficulties, or personnel problems. I'm not saying that you have to do everything on your own, but you need to be able to rely on yourself to get things done.

As a business owner, you can't always rely on others to get things done. You have to be able to do it yourself. That's why it's important to have a wide range of skills. You need to be able to market your business, manage finances, and provide customer service, among other things. Of course, you can't be expected to be an expert in everything. But if you're able to handle the basics, it will go a long way toward ensuring the success of your business. I know from experience that it's not always easy to do everything yourself. But if you're dedicated and willing to put in the hard work, it's certainly possible. And in the end, it's often worth it. There's no greater satisfaction than knowing that you've built something from the ground up – and that you did it all yourself.

This means you're going to have to be organized, set priorities, and know when to ask for help. By taking the time to develop a strong work ethic and learning how to manage your time effectively, you'll be setting yourself up for success as a business owner.

In order to become a more self-reliant business owner, it is important to first focus on your own personal development.

This means taking the time to learn new skills and knowledge and to grow as an individual. You can do this by:
- Making an effort to educate yourself about all aspects of your business.
- Read industry news, attend conferences, and regularly meet with your team to discuss the latest developments. This will help you to form your own opinions and make informed decisions.
- Learning new skills. There's no need to be an expert at everything, but it helps to have a basic understanding of the most essential aspects of running your business.
- Delegating or outsourcing tasks you're not good at or that take up too much of your time. This will free up your time so you can focus on what you do best.
- Creating systems and procedures. Having set processes in place for how things are done will help to ensure that things run smoothly even when you're not there. And if something does go wrong, you'll be able to quickly identify and correct the issue.
- Listening to your intuition. We all have an inner voice that can guide us, but we often ignore it in favor of logic or common sense. The next time you're facing a tough decision, take a step back and ask yourself what feels right.

By following these simple tips, you can start to become more self-reliant and build a stronger foundation for your business.

Being an entrepreneur can be a lonely road. You are the one in charge of your own success or failure. However, it is important to remember that you have what it takes. Use the gifts God gave you to be your own village. If you're extroverted, find a mentor who can teach you and help you navigate the early stages of running your business. Or join an entrepreneur meetup group so you can bounce ideas off other like-minded individuals. If you're more of an introvert like me, reflect and think deeply. Write things down. Read books and online content to help boost your knowledge. Study those who have already achieved what you're looking to do.

Whatever your gifts are, don't be afraid to be your own village. You have what it takes to bring your dreams of entrepreneurship to life.

Sometimes you have to go at it alone.

7
YOU NEED A STRONG, DETERMINED, AND PERSISTENT MIND

"If you can't fly, then run, if you can't run then walk if you can't walk then crawl, but whatever you do you have to keep moving forward." - Martin Luther King, Jr.

Even though I consider myself a pretty self-reliant person, there were several days throughout my entrepreneurship journey, when I wanted to give up. But I knew that I could do that. If I gave up, I was giving up on my kids and the boys and girls in my community, and I wasn't going to do that. My desire to serve and help them kept me going.

Entrepreneurship isn't always going to be easy, so you need to think about what you're going to do when things go bad. Because no matter how great your idea is or how strong your support system is, things will go bad at some point. But you've got to stay strong. The journey and the reward are worth it.

You've got to have grit, which for me, means standing strong and staying the course. You're going to face challenges as an aspiring business owner and it will be so easy to give up when things get tough. But research has found that the most successful people achieve their goals because they have grit. Being talented and intelligent are good, but they don't always lead to success. Grit, determination, and perseverance do.

Grit is the ability to keep going when you face setbacks. Grit means sticking with something even when it's difficult. It's about setting your sights on a goal and not giving up, no matter the obstacles you face. People with grit aren't successful because they're talented or lucky. They're successful because they're willing to put in the hard work needed to reach their goal. People with grit believe that they can overcome any obstacle. That's the kind of mindset you need to have if you're an aspiring entrepreneur or business owner.

When you have a resilient mindset, you view challenges as opportunities for growth and view failures as stepping stones to success. Resilient people are also able to withstand stress and adversity because they have a mindset of strength and determination.

So how can you develop a resilient mindset? You can learn to reframe your thinking. When you catch yourself wondering "why me?" or feeling sorry for yourself, stop and remind yourself that this is just a temporary setback.

This mindset shift will help you to better cope with difficult times and come out stronger on the other side. Another way to develop resilience is through self-care. Taking care of yourself physically, emotionally, and mentally will help to build your inner strength and fortitude. When you nurture yourself, you are better equipped to handle whatever life throws your way. Lastly, write down affirmations. When I was struggling to keep going, the number one affirmation I wrote down was "she believed she could so she did." To this day, I live by that affirmation.

It wasn't always easy, but I am happy to say that I am actually living out the affirmations I used to write down. Even now, on my wall, I have a poster saying, "positive mind, positive vibes, positive life." I'm not perfect, but that's how I live my life.

I take life as it comes. I do what I can to stay positive. And I refuse to give up on myself. That's the mindset I want each and every one of my girls at Women of Sure Sertainity to have.

Having a determined and persistent mind is everything.

John Maxwell and I at the August 2022 IMC Orlando, FL

The John Maxwell Team and I at the IMC August 2022 Orlando, FL

8
NEVER STOP BUILDING

"The best way to predict the future is to create it." - Abraham Lincoln

Along with having a persistent mind, you should never stop building. There is no finish line in entrepreneurship. If you want to be one of the most successful business owners, you should always be looking for new opportunities to grow and expand. You should always be on the lookout for new ideas, products, and ways to reach your target market. Continue to innovate new things and experiment with new ways to take your business to the next level.

At times, this relentlessness can be exhausting, but it separates the successful from the unsuccessful. As an entrepreneur, I've learned that complacency is the enemy of progress. I am always looking to improve my skills and business ventures. I am always looking to push forward and strive for more.

That's why on top of starting my credit repair business, I created a mentoring organization. But I didn't stop there. I've gone on to get my real estate license and have become a certified John Maxwell team member. And my plans for the future are even bigger.

In the future, I see myself in a different country - Brazil or Australia. I'm at a beautiful hotel or retreat and I am teaching older adults about business and John Maxwell's The 15 Invaluable Laws Of Growth. I'm motivating them. Sure, I get nervous thinking about standing up in front of large crowds of people, but I remind myself to never stop building.

Entrepreneurship is about being perfect. It's about connecting with people, talking with them, and providing them goods, services, and information they need.

Future leaders, we have to keep the world going. One of the best ways to do that is to share knowledge. If you've got the knowledge in you, get it out there so the world can hear it. You are important and the world needs to know what you have to say and what you have to offer.

That's what I taught my children and all of them have started to build and develop their own businesses.

My son O'Neil is only 26 years old, but he has his own trucking company. He also has an Airbnb in Texas that he started as a business venture as well. Even though he's quite successful, he hasn't stopped building. Right now, he's in the process of getting more trucks. If he gets more trucks, he can hire more drivers and have them work the business, which frees him up to do other things. There are other businesses he wants to start such as a new clothing line. He also wants to get more Airbnbs in the future.

My other son, Omar, is 24, and he has his own rental car company. He has a couple of cars that he rents out. He also works for BMW as a salesman.

Oneika, my oldest daughter, is in college studying to be a pharmacist.

My daughter Kayla is a notary. I am in the process of getting her a google page to market her business and start getting clients. Right now, she primarily provides her services to friends and family since she's in college studying to be an anesthesiologist assistant. She's not very entrepreneurial, but at least she's starting the process and getting in the mindset of having multiple streams of income.

Wherever you are now and whatever your dreams are, don't stop building. God gave you that vision, that dream, and your purpose just for you. The people around you will not understand at times why or what you are doing. Guess what it is not for them to know or understand God didn't give them your vision, dream, or purpose he only gave that to you. While you are on your journey to whatever your success looks like at the end for you, you will lose family, friends, and associates along the way you will feel lonely, tired, frustrated, and want to give up but I am here to tell you DON'T GIVE UP. KEEP GOING.

The people who are meant to be in your life will come either for a reason or a season or someone who will just come to give that extra boost when you need it the most or even this book you are reading now. Most of all, believe in yourself. Be your biggest cheerleader. Get out of your own way. Block out the negativity in your own head, and don't listen to little you. Listen to big you. That's the version of yourself that has big dreams and larger-than-life aspirations. The world needs to know who you are and what you have to offer. Success is on the other side of yes and when you feel like quitting always remember your why. No matter what you face or find yourself enduring, never, ever stop building.

Remember, the best way to determine your future is to create it. The power to change your life and the lives of others is in your hands.

6 TOUGH (BUT TRUE) LESSONS ABOUT BUSINESS

She Believed She Could So She Did.

StoryTerrace

www.ingramcontent.com/pod-product-compliance
Lightning Source LLC
LaVergne TN
LVHW061622070526
838199LV00078B/7385